The UNIVERSE'S GREATEST

SCHOOL JOKES

and RIP-ROARING RIDDLES

Artie Bennett

STERLING CHILDREN'S BOOKS

New York

To teachers and librarians everywhere,
those unsung heroes whose contribution is
beyond measure

STERLING CHILDREN'S BOOKS
New York

An Imprint of Sterling Publishing Co., Inc.
1166 Avenue of the Americas
New York. NY 10036

ISBN 978-1-4549-2985-7

Distributed in Canada by Sterling Publishing Co., Inc.
c/o Canadian Manda Group, 664 Annette Street
Toronto, Ontario M6S 2C8, Canada
Distributed in the United Kingdom by GMC Distribution Services
Castle Place, 166 High Street, Lewes, East Sussex BN7 1XU, England
Distributed in Australia by NewSouth Books
University of New South Wales, Sydney, NSW 2052, Australia

For information about custom editions, special sales, and premium and
corporate purchases, please contact Sterling Special Sales at 800-805-5489 or
specialsales@sterlingpublishing.com.
Manufactured in Canada

Lot #:
2 4 6 8 10 9 7 5 3 1
05/19

sterlingpublishing.com

Cover illustration by Julie Robine
Cover and interior art components by iStock and Shutterstock
Cover and interior design by Julie Robine

Contents

SCHOOLED IN HUMOR

Which of the school supplies is in charge of all the others?

The ruler.

Where do the brightest members of a school of fish go after graduation?

A think tank!

What do you call an overcrowded one-room schoolhouse?

A *no-*room schoolhouse!

LEAH: Do teddy bears do well on their exams?
ARTIE: Yes, they often get an A-plush!

Which class has great appeal for rowdy students?

*Anti*social studies.

What is three feet long and found just outside the school?

A school yard!

What writing instruments were used for the science lesson on animal excretion?

Number 2 pencils.

What do houseplants bring home from school that shows their parents how well they did?

Their *repot* cards.

Where do clams learn their ABCs?

Shell-ementary school.

What do the highest-achieving students spread butter on for breakfast?

An honor roll.

What's the large assembly room where students often fall asleep called?

An audi-snorium.

Why was the class hamster treated with special favor?

She was the teacher's pet.

What's one part of the school play called?

A class act.

Why is the entranceway to the New York Public Library flanked by two huge marble lions?

So you can read between the lions!

What did the less-than-studious dolphins get on their exam?

High seas.

What type of exam features famous fathers from history?

A *pop* quiz.

What do students get from staying up all night cramming for an exam?

Schoolbags under their eyes.

How did the students feel when they were greeted with a surprise exam?

Testy!

Who kept watch over ancient Greek and Roman children traveling to and from school?

Crossing gods.

What do pirates love to study?

Arrrrt!

Why was the disruptive boy hanging from the basketball hoop?

He was suspended.

What grades do flower pollinators usually get?

Bs.

In what grade do budding biologists study the excretory system?

Turd grade.

Why did the student bring a tortoise to class?

It was for show-and-shell.

Why doesn't the sun need to go to college?

It already has millions of degrees.

Where did Sherlock Holmes and Watson first meet?

Elementary school.

ARTIE: Did you hear about the girl who was headed to class in a windstorm?

LEAH: Mm-hmm. She was blown off course.

What is it called when your candy bar has snapped in two?

A snack break.

How do the smartest students travel overseas to study?

On a scholar ship!

Why do music school students need hammers and ladders?

To help them hit the high notes.

What grade does a very smart horse get?

A neigh-plus.

What do you get when you sneeze during homeroom?

Homesick.

Who is apt to tell fibs in school?

The lie-brarian.

Why did the teacher bring high-wattage bulbs to school?

Because her class was rather dim.

HA HA HA HA HA HA HA HA

In which competitions do students have to identify items by their aroma?

Smelling bees.

What's the perfect breakfast food to eat before English class?

An English muffin.

Why did the teacher give the lesson in front of the window?

She wanted it to be clear.

Where do you record notes about the circus?

In a three-ring binder.

LEAH: I hear you have a very good chemistry teacher.

ARTIE: Yes, he has all the right elements.

Which head of school can *never* be defeated?

An invincible principal.

When did middle schools achieve their greatest popularity?

In the Middle Ages.

HA HA HA HA HA

How would you describe an academy located on a mountaintop?

A *high* school.

What did the overaggressive player use to beat his opponent in a board game?

A chess club.

Where was Sir Lancelot educated?

Knight school.

What types of schools exert a bad influence?

Ones without *principals*.

Why do magicians prosper in school?

They're good with trick questions.

What television station can help you with your English lessons?

The English Channel!

ARTIE: Did you learn a lot in school today?

LEAH: Apparently, not enough. I have to go back tomorrow!

Why was the Cyclops engaged in one-on-one learning?

He had only one pupil.

Knock, knock.

Who's there?

Ida.

Ida who?

Ida gotten better grades if only I'd studied more!

What do you call a schoolboy taking a second-period class?

A second-class citizen.

Why did the teacher put the tests in a food processor?

She was grating the exams.

What did the pen say to the pencil?

"I see your point!"

Which breed of dog will retrieve your lost laptop?

The computer Lab.

What did the eraser say to the clumsy student?

"You rub me the wrong way."

HA HA

What do you call a student who flunks ballet?

A dance dunce.

Why do farts never finish out the school year?

Because they always get expelled!

Which annual publication records all the school slang?

The yeah-book.

Which field of study examines snakes through the ages?

Hiss-tory.

Which kind of teacher always has a foot-long sandwich for lunch?

A sub.

ARTIE: I got a 100 in school today!
LEAH: Wonderful news! In what?
ARTIE: A 50 in reading and a 50 in math.

Which animal becomes a copycat during exams?

The cheetah.

What do teachers cover their mattresses with?

Worksheets.

ARTIE: Did you hear about the student who flunked driving school?

LEAH: Yes, I did. He thought it was a crash course.

In what class do you learn the science behind soda?

Fizz Ed.

Where did Carly earn first prize on her zombie biology project?

The science fear.

Why is a school for ruffians so disorganized?

It has no class.

What did the young turtles tell their teacher to express their appreciation?

"You tortoise everything we know."

How do squids get to school?

By octobus.

Where does a cad go to school?

Academy.

Who exercises the highest authority in the insect kingdom?

The monarch butterfly.

How did the blackboard feel about being replaced by a smartboard?

It chalked it up to changing times.

What do you call a malfunctioning smartboard?

A stupidboard.

Which class studies the science behind making purchases?

Buy-ology.

What happened to the easel in the chem lab?

It went "Pop! Goes the Easel."

What do you call it when a toilet explodes?

A bathroom break.

Where do surfers learn their craft?

Boarding school.

Why did the girl bring scissors to school?

She wanted to cut class.

ARTIE: Do elves have to learn their ABCs?

LEAH: Sure! Haven't you heard of the elf-abet?

What do the children of architects prefer to write on?

Construction paper.

Why did the boy take his schoolwork aboard the airplane?

He wanted a higher education.

Who helps you learn to play the flute outside of school?

A private tooter.

What is easier to crack when you put on a frock or gown?

A dress code.

Why is it difficult to learn to throw a curveball?

It has a steep learning curve.

LEAH: Wake up, Artie. Wake up. You're late for school.

ARTIE: But I don't wanna go. The kids all make fun of me. And the teachers pick on me.

LEAH: But you *have* to go. *You're* the principal!

What is it called when you're learning how to tell time?

A teachable moment.

What's the best way to get straight As?

Use a ruler!

What do you call a French teacher who makes a good living?

A French breadwinner.

Which items of neckwear are handed down from student to student?

Old school ties.

ARTIE: Did you hear about the student with terrible breath?

LEAH: Yes, he was in a class by himself.

How would you describe the United Nations school?

World class.

What comes after you flunk your ABCs?

Ds.

HA HA HA HA HA

TEACHER: Did your mother help you with your homework?

ARTIE: No, she did it all by herself.

Which buzzing insects do well in the language arts?

Spelling bees.

What do English teachers have for lunch?

Alphabet soup.

What can you use in an emergency if you tear your kilt?

Scotch tape.

Who holds the all-time record for missing the most school?

Captain Hooky.

Where do pencils come from?

Pencil-vania.

Knock, knock.

Who's there?

Ahmed.

Ahmed who?

Ahmed an A-plus on the test! How'd you do?

Which animals make the most sensible teachers?

Skunks—because they make a lot of *scents*.

What do the finest dental school students get?

A plaque.

Which schools exert a powerful attraction for students?

Magnet schools.

What do hungry slackers turn into?

Snackers!

What does the football team take notes in?

Spiral notebooks.

Where do you learn nursery rhymes?

Nursery school.

ARTIE: Do cows excel in school?

LEAH: Haven't you heard of grade-A beef?

What's another word for "to spend too much time in the bathroom"?

Stall.

HA HA HA HA HA HA HA HA

Who cleans up spilled custard in the lunchroom?

The custardian.

What do cheerleaders say when they want a better grade?

"Gimme an A!"

Why was the teacher forced to wear sunglasses during class?

She had very bright students.

Where does fourth grade come after fifth grade?

In the dictionary!

In what school do you have to drop out to graduate?

Skydiving school!

What do you call the part of a lock that's received its diploma?

A graduated cylinder.

What was the cow's favorite class?

Moo-sic.

Who teaches the grandchildren good grammar?

Gramma!

What do schools in cowboy country have?

Homerooms on the range.

What do you call it when you pass a tough history exam?

Surviving the test of time.

How do students pay to better develop their instincts?

In-tuition.

Who advises and trains younger students on the proper way to bully one another?

A tor-*mentor*!

What do you do if your teacher rolls her eyes at you?

Roll them back to her.

What do you call curricula that are more than you need to graduate?

Extra curricula!

Who teaches us about our brain, eyes, ears, and more?

The head teacher.

LEAH: You've heard of the grammar police, right? Well, who makes sure that you're using the right words?

ARTIE: The vocabulary constabulary!

Which educational method teaches your parrot language skills through the mastery of sounds?

Polly Phonics!

Why was the school closed when the singer Phoebe Snow was set to perform?

They took a Snow day.

What do you have if you're knowledgeable about liquid metric measurements?

Liter-acy.

TEACHER: Leah, can you show us where America is on the map?

LEAH: Yes, here it is.

TEACHER: Very good. Now, class, can you tell me who found America?

CLASS: Leah did!

Where is a home-schooled student taught?

Homeroom!

HA

Why did the class seem unusually long?

It was the lesson of a lifetime.

Where do you learn to make scrumptious ice cream dishes?

Sundae school.

What is the limit placed on all purchases by simpleminded students called?

A dunce cap.

Where do educational reformers get their start?

Reform school.

What did the girl who was struggling with her French lessons fear she would become?

French toast!

What do you call an especially energetic prep school?

A pep school.

How are children transported to a charter school?

By charter bus.

When is a school bus *not* a school bus?

When it turns in to the parking lot.

Who gives you instruction on the proper way to pass gas?

A tooter!

What do you need to use the bathroom at boarding school?

A boarding pass.

What did the debate between two classes turn into?

Class warfare.

Knock, knock.

Who's there?

Police.

Police who?

Police be my study partner! I need to ace tomorrow's exam!

GO TEAM!

THE CAFETERIA: SERVED WITH A SIDE OF SILLINESS

What did the klutzy boy say when he dropped his trayful of food in his lap?

"Hey, everybody. Lunch is on me!"

Why did the girl pack a flashlight in her lunchbox?

She wanted a light lunch.

What is a great ape's favorite snack with milk?

Chocolate chimp cookies.

What is a sea turtle's favorite sandwich?

Peanut butter and jellyfish.

What entrée *always* gives vampire students heartburn?

Steak.

What is the world's longest fruit?

Banananananananananananananana.

Which breakfast dish is made with illegally obtained items?

Poached eggs.

What do you call students who have gorged themselves in the cafeteria?

Dilated pupils.

LEAH: I have a terrible fear of cleaning my teeth after I eat.

ARTIE: Sounds like a bad case of floss-trophobia.

Which vegetables shoot out green juice when you bite into them?

Brussels spouts.

Why do teddy bears never visit the cafeteria?

They're already stuffed.

Which sandwich do you get when the lunch lady slaps ground beef on your open hamburger bun?

A slappy joe.

And what sandwich is great for trading among classmates?

A swappy joe.

What is an octopus's favorite dessert?

A crab cake.

ARTIE: Do you like that melted cheese dish from Switzerland?

LEAH: I'm fond of fondue.

Which sandwich is best eaten frozen?

An ice cream sandwich.

Where do dogs eat during lunch break?

The cafeterrier.

What does the school basketball team love to eat?

Swish kebab.

What's the worst thing you're likely to find in the school cafeteria?

The food!

What is a bully's favorite meat snack?

Beef jerky.

What do you call a schoolboy who stumbles into a vat of goulash in the cafeteria?

A stew-dent.

Why do burgers taste better in outer-space school?

They're *meteor*.

What do you call students who eat only triangular-shaped pieces of cheese?

Wedge-atarians.

Why is pasta considered "brain food"?

Because you're using your noodle.

What do traitors eat before school?

Eggs Benedict Arnold.

Which vegetable do you never want to fall on your head?

Squash.

LEAH: Did you hear about the student who grew highly excitable about a popular Japanese fried food?

ARTIE: Yes, he became *very* tempura-mental.

What was it called when two lobsters in the pot began battling each other?

A food fight!

What does the chess club have for lunch?

A chess club sandwich.

Which lettuce dish can give one fits?

A seizure salad.

Why was the clock in the cafeteria always a little slow?

Because it went back four seconds.

What's a cannibal's favorite cafeteria dessert?

Ladyfingers.

What did the rabbit say to the carrot?

"It's been nice gnawing you."

HA HA HA

Why is the cantaloupe so popular?

It's one in a melon.

What do you call microwavable potato chips?

Microchips.

Which luncheon meat do class clowns prefer?

Baloney.

Which breakfast dish is hard to beat?

Hard-boiled eggs.

LEAH: Why doesn't anyone joke about the cafeteria pizza?

ARTIE: Because it's too cheesy.

What do meditators love to eat for breakfast?

An *ommmmm*-lette.

When should you keep a close watch on your cheese?

When it's up to no Gouda.

Which English statesman invented cured breakfast meat?

Sir Francis Bacon.

Why do oranges do so well in school?

They can concentrate.

What do adorable students like for dessert?

Cutey-pie.

Which pasta dish causes acne?

Ziti.

What do you call a chickpea that's all washed up?

A has-bean!

Who's in charge of the dairy section in the school cafeteria?

The big cheese.

Which cafeteria food is best before naptime?

PiZZZZZZZZZZa.

Why do gingersnaps always make a fuss?

Because that's the way the cookie grumbles.

ARTIE: Can a lettuce be a lawyer?

LEAH: Sure, but not until it passes the salad bar.

How did the cookie do on the test?

The results were crummy.

Which little pastry costs a great deal of money?

A small fortune cookie.

How do you repair a damaged tomato?

With tomato paste!

What do you call mock macaroni?

An impasta!

HA HA HA HA

Why don't lunch ladies take criticism easily?

Because they can dish it out, but they can't take it.

Which spicy meat dish is good to have when you're feeling a little cold?

Chili.

Why should you never leave alphabet soup unattended on the stove?

Because it can spell disaster.

How do you transform a pot of gold into a pot of soup?

Add twenty-four carrots.

Which cafeteria sandwich is prepared with power tools?

Drilled cheese.

What was Moby Dick's favorite food?

Fish and ships.

LEAH: Why are there little hairs in my nutty green ice cream?

ARTIE: What's the matter? Didn't you order mustachio?

What do you call a cow without legs?

Ground beef.

Why was the thin cracker in tears?

Because its mother was a wafer so long.

What do you call a bout of laughter brought on by a cup of coffee?

A brew-ha-ha.

Which dessert cleans your tummy after you eat it?

Sponge cake.

What do you call a lazy baby marsupial?

A pouch potato.

What happened to the tomato that slept on the job?

He got canned.

ARTIE: What is the most sacred cheese?

LEAH: Swiss. Because it's holey.

What do you call 2,000 pounds of Chinese soup?

Won-ton.

HA HA HA HA HA
HA HA HA HA HA

Why does yogurt listen to classical music while studying?

Because it's cultured.

What do the school cafeterias serve in South Korea?

Seoul food!

Where do bats eat their lunch at school?

The cave-eteria.

Where is the funniest place in school?

The laugheteria!

NO LAUGHING IN THE LIBRARY

ARTIE: Do kids enjoy reading books about Thanksgiving and turkeys?

LEAH: Yes, they gobble them up!

Which classic children's book series was based on the memories of a small rodent growing up in the Midwest?

Little Mouse on the Prairie.

What profession did the girl who never returned her library books go into?

Bookkeeping!

Which beloved children's book writer is viewed by many readers as practically a god?

Dr. Zeus.

What has a spine yet no bones?

A book!

ARTIE: If Liberians are from Liberia, where are librarians from?
LEAH: Libraria?
ARTIE: No, it depends where they were born.
LEAH: Oh.

What are librarians' favorite green vegetables?

Quiet peas.

What do you call two knights sharing a book?

On the same page.

When the simpleton was told by his teacher to "hit the books," what did he use?

A book club!

Where are you most likely to slip in the library?

In the non-friction section.

Knock, knock.

Who's there?

Rita.

Rita who?

Rita good book lately?

HA HA HA HA HA

How do you know when a book is excited?

When its circulation increases.

What do librarians put on when they're feeling cold?

A book jacket.

ARTIE: I loved reading that textbook about anti-gravity.

LEAH: Yeah, I heard you couldn't put it down!

Where do librarians sleep?

Between the covers.

Why do magicians make such good readers?

They know every trick in the book.

What did the hen say to the librarian?

I'm sorry. I forgot to return my book-book-book.

Which classic fantasy centered around a saber that was safeguarded in an oven?

The Sword in the Stove.

Do mummies enjoy a good book?

Yes, they like to get wrapped up in it.

Where can you find books about assorted small fruit?

In the li-berry!

Why couldn't the student visit the library?

It was completely booked.

What's the best way to contact a book?

Page it!

Which book lists and defines all the blessings from A to Z?

A benediction-ary.

Why are libraries so tall?

They have a lot of stories.

Which children's novel told the story of the barn spider who invented the Internet?

Charlotte's Web.

Why did the T. rex avoid the library?

Because his books were 65 million years overdue!

What did the hipster say to the librarian?

"Can you tell me if my book is over, dude?"

Which Shakespearean play details a young woman's tragic love for roping and bronc riding?

Rodeo and Juliet.

What's the best way to get to know a book?

Check it out!

Knock, knock.

Who's there?

Voodoo.

Voodoo who?

Voodoo you think you are not returning your library books?

Which are the loudest books?

The ones with many volumes.

What is a librarian's favorite color?

Well, red.

What did the library detective solve?

Book cases.

Which literary character wakes up from a long sleep with his face lined with age?

Rip Van Wrinkle.

Why was the clock removed from the school library?

It *tocked* too loud.

Which sweat-jacketed folk hero robbed from the rich and gave to the poor?

Robin Hoodie.

Which classic novel told the story of a catfish growing up along the Mississippi River?

The Adventures of Huckleberry Fin.

What was Peter Pan called when he soared through the air?

A flying Pan.

Why did the girl eventually stop reading *The Lord of the Rings*?

She kicked the hobbit.

Which classic story features a farm girl named Dorothy who goes on an adventure with her pet chameleon?

The Wonderful Lizard of Oz.

Which essential wordbook contains entries that conflict with each other?

A contradiction-ary.

What happened when the librarian threw her old books in the sea?

A title wave.

Which fantasy series features a boy who is a wizard with ceramic ware?

Harry Pottery.

What do wise, old owls like to eat?

Bookworms.

ARITHMETICKLES

What is the circumference of an apple divided by its diameter?

Apple pi!

What's the most adorable thing you'll find in geometry?

Acute angle.

LEAH: If Sam had forty donuts and ate nine of them, what would he have?

ARTIE: A bellyache!

Why is a nose, even a large one, never twelve inches long?

Because then it would be a foot!

What did the geometrist cry out when her parrot escaped out the window?

"Polly gone!"

Where do rectangles that misbehave often wind up?

In prism.

What do you call a right angle that gives bad advice?

A wrong angle.

Why did the math book look worried?

It had a lot of problems.

How do you know that math teachers love humanity?

Because they make sure that everyone counts.

Which wise bird excels at math?

The owl-gebra.

Where do math teachers eat their lunch?

At a times table.

How do you turn a seven into an even number?

Remove the *s*!

What candy snack is suitable for geometry class?

Measure mints.

Why did the geometry teacher call in sick?

He twisted his angle.

What is the most popular New York City tourist attraction for math teachers?

Times Square.

Why do triangles avoid discussions with circles?

They find them pointless.

What did the math teacher name her parrot?

Polly Nomial.

How would you describe someone who is very attentive to the details of math?

Arith-meticulous.

Which curved sailing ship is mentioned in the Bible?

Noah's Arc.

Why do three and five act so bizarrely?

They're odd numbers.

Why do geometry teachers make great reporters?

They can cover a story from many angles.

HA HA HA HA HA
HA HA HA HA HA

What do you get when a lion is chasing you but you stop to add 4 + 4?

Ate!

What do you call nomadic numbers?

Roamin' numerals.

Which sea creature is good at addition?

The octoplus.

Where do you buy a ruler that is three feet long?

At a yard sale.

Which shape was in a car accident?

The wrecked-angle.

Why was the obtuse angle perspiring?

It was over ninety degrees.

What did the potted plant in math class have?

Square roots.

Why do math teachers eat small portions?

They're always watching their figures.

Who performs astounding feats with numbers?

A mathemagician.

What did the square say to the circle?

"Been around long?"

Why did the math teacher place a ruler alongside his pillow?

He wanted to see how long he slept.

Which is the hardest shape to escape from?

The trap-ezoid.

ARTIE: If you have ten apples in one hand and ten pears in the other, what do you have?

LEAH: Huge hands!

Why does a dime do better on tests than a nickel?

Because it has more cents.

Why were the geometry students tired all the time?

They were all out of shape.

Which knight built the famous Round Table?

Sir Cumference.

HA HA HA HA HA

When everything goes wrong, what can you always count on?

Your fingers!

ARTIE: What's twigonometry?
LEAH: A "branch" of mathematics!

Which little bloodsuckers attach themselves to math teachers?

Arithme-ticks!

MIRTH SCIENCE

Why should you never believe an atom?

They make up everything.

ARTIE: Everyone knows that H_2O is the chemical formula for water. But what's the chemical formula for ice?
LEAH: H_2O cubed!

Why are chemists great at problem-solving?

They have all the solutions.

Which chemical element was discovered by a boring moron?

Boron!

What would you get when King Arthur farted?

A noble gas.

Why are protons so optimistic?

They have a positive nature.

Which branch of science is filled with surprise over changing national borders?

Gee-ography!

How do astronomers organize a party?

They planet.

Knock, knock.

Who's there?

Element.

Element who?

Element no harm. She's sorry.

ARTIE: What is the most important thing to know in chemistry class?

LEAH: Never lick the spoon!

HA HA HA HA HA HA HA HA HA

What do astronomers get in their well-worn black socks?

Black holes.

Why was the biologist upset with his roommate?

He wouldn't wash the Petri dishes.

LEAH: Do you know the difference between a dog and a marine biologist?

ARTIE: Yes, a dog wags a tail, but a marine biologist tags a whale.

Where do rocket ships pay to dock at space stations?

At parking meteors.

What does a statistician say to her dog?

"Data boy!"

Why are chemists so fond of nitrates?

They're cheaper than day rates.

What do you call an unpopular climatologist?

An absolute zero.

Why can't neutrons use a credit card?

They have no charge.

How do you know who your cousins are?

The theory of relativity.

ARTIE: If H_2O is water, what's H_2O_4?
LEAH: Drinking, washing, swimming, bathing, and putting out fires.

Where do the chemistry teachers eat their lunch?

At the periodic table.

LEAH: Did you hear about the magnets that were quarreling?
ARTIE: They were poles apart.

How do you know a scientist likes you?

She has her ion you.

What does a duck who has studied physics say?

"Quark, quark!"

HA HA HA HA HA

Who works alongside a Labrador retriever in chemistry class?

A Lab partner.

When should biologists never acquire a cell?

After its cell-by date.

Which religious group uses the scientific method?

Scientific Methodists.

What did Marie Curie feel when she was out on a disappointing date?

No chemistry!

Why was the noble gas so sad?

Because all her friends argon.

What do marine biology teachers like to do?

Test the waters.

HA HA HA HA HA HA HA HA

What did Massachusetts colonists have a desperate need for after drinking too much tea?

A Boston tea potty.

What did Noah equip the ark with for night travel?

Floodlights.

Who was the young chicken who befriended Robin Hood?

Fryer Tuck.

Which famous French emperor met an explosive end?

Napoleon Blown Apart.

LEAH: How do we know that the heroes who established the United States of America were abandoned as children?

ARTIE: Haven't you heard of the Foundling Fathers?

HA HA HA
HA HA HA HA HA

What lullaby would Russian parents sing to their sons, who would grow up to be great leaders?

"Twinkle, Twinkle, Little Tsar."

Where did the Pilgrim women keep their powder puffs?

In the Mayflower Compact.

Which colonial governing body was known for its frequent bathroom breaks?

The Incontinental Congress.

What do Alexander the Great and Dora the Explorer share?

The same middle name.

Which larger-than-life American folk hero suffered from a disorder of the big toe?

Paul Bunion.

How did the Vikings communicate from their longships?

By Norse code.

Where did King Arthur, who studied hard for his exams, build his castle?

Cram-a-lot!

What was the Pilgrims' favorite type of music?

Plymouth Rock.

Which fabled leader founded the Mongol Empire through trickery and deception?

Genghis Con.

Where was fried food invented?

Ancient Grease.

What was Attila's pet name for his wife?

Hon.

Why did the tourist feel disappointed upon seeing the Liberty Bell?

It wasn't all it was cracked up to be.

What did pirates from Texas wear on their heads?

Ten-galleon hats.

HA HA HA HA HA
HA HA HA HA HA
HA HA HA HA HA

Who was the heroic Frenchwoman who escaped religious persecution by stowing away on a biblical ship?

Joan of Ark.

What did the colonial dentists implant in our first president's mouth when his wooden teeth finally wore out?

The George Washington bridge.

What would Sir Lancelot say at bedtime?

"Knighty-knight."

Which famous twelfth-century British document guaranteed the unrestricted flow of lava?

The Magma Carta.

What was President Lincoln's favorite class pet?

Abrahamster.

In which course can we learn a lot about the Declaration of Independence on our own?

Independent studies.

What was it called when Iceland fought Greenland?

A cold war.

Why didn't the
early colonists get
out there and vote?

They lacked
the constitution
for it.

What document
did ducks create to
guarantee freedom from
some hunting practices?

A Bill of Rights.

How do you determine
how old an astronaut is?

From their Space
Age.

How did Ben Franklin
feel when he discovered
electricity?

He was shocked.

Which British king
assisted one of the participants at
all the royal duels?

George the Second.

GYM DANDIES

In which class do students often sweat so much you're likely to hear "P.U.!"?

P.E.

Where do schools of fish change for gym class?

Davy Jones's locker room.

LEAH: Did the swim class go well?
ARTIE: Yes, swimmingly!

Which insects are always excused from gym class?

Millipedes, because they can't afford the sneakers.

What sport do vampires come out for?

Casketball.

What do you aim at when playing dodgeball?

A student body.

Which racquet sport is just no good to play?

Bad-minton!

What did students in ancient Rome wear for yoga class?

A yoga toga.

Why don't members of the swim team show up for practice on rainy days?

They don't want to get wet.

Why do bananas excel in gym class?

They make great banana splits.

Which basketball shot can you put money into?

A bank shot.

What do legumes become in gym class?

Runner beans.

What does the swim team eat their lunch on?

Pool tables.

Why do pigs need to pass more when playing basketball?

To keep from becoming ball hogs.

Which team sport that uses a net is often played between two mountains?

Valleyball.

What's the favorite exercise of certain playing cards?

Jumping jacks.

What do you call a canine umpire?

A ruffaree.

Why were the twin babies banned from the basketball game?

They kept double dribbling.

What do exaggerators do in yoga class?

They stretch the truth.

Where do fish like to hang out in school?

The swim-nasium.

ARTIE: Did you hear about the runner who froze up whenever he had to jump a hurdle?
LEAH: Yeah, but he got over it.

Why do skunks hate gym class?

The lockers stink.

How do ghosts stay in shape?

They exorcise.

Why did the simpleton stop eating before the basketball game?

He heard there would be a fast break during the game.

What sport were the kids who skipped school playing?

They were playing hooky!

Why are basketball players so cool?

They play surrounded by fans.

Which dogs can be taught to roll with the punches?

Boxers!

What did the boy say when someone noticed he wasn't perspiring after a vigorous run?

"No sweat!"

Where do the students at driving school head during gym class?

The carpool.

What game do some cars like to play?

Dodge ball.

ARTIE: When is a basketball like a donut?
LEAH: When it's dunked!

ALL PETS ARE OFF

Why did the class pet report a student she saw cheating?

She was a tattlesnake.

What does the class's pet frog eat with its hamburgers?

French flies.

Where do mice deposit their savings?

Cheese Manhattan Bank.

HA HA HA HA HA

Which classroom pet is housed in the teachers' lounge?

The teachers' lounge lizard.

Why did the little insect stay away from school?

He was a true-ant.

ARTIE: Do snakes love joke and riddle books?

LEAH: Yes, they find them hiss-terical.

Which class do fish take in school?

They take de-bate.

Which European city do hamsters come from?

Hamsterdam.

ARTIE: Did you see the classified ad that the parrot placed for someone to break into his owner's safe?

LEAH: Yes, it said "Polly want a cracker!"

HA HA HA HA HA HA HA HA HA HA

Knock, knock.

> Who's there?

Iguana.

> Iguana who?

Iguana be your boyfriend!

What do snakes do after a brawl?

> They hiss and make up.

Why do tadpoles have trouble wearing glasses?

> Because they keep *frogging* up.

What does a mouse say to another after a visit?

> "Thank you for droppings by."

What does the rooster tell his chicks when they return home from school?

> "Cock-a-doodle-*doooo* your homework."

How does a snake finish off a love letter?

> He seals it with a hiss.

How would you describe a frog with a broken leg?

> Unhoppy!

HA HA HA

Which snake makes a great kindergarten classroom pet?

A kinder-garter snake!

What do you call a courteous snake?

A civil serpent.

Why couldn't the fly see anything?

She was lost in a frog.

How does a small rodent revive another when it's passed out?

With mouse-to-mouse resuscitation.

Who watches over all the geckos and skinks?

The monitor lizard.

Where can you find ants milking aphids?

On an ant farm.

Why did the rabbit build an aboveground house?

He was fed up with the hole thing.

Why did the hamster quit his job as school pet?

He felt the celery was too low.

HA HA HA
HA HA HA

What do rabbits need after being caught out in the rain?

A hare dryer.

Which snake can erect buildings?

The boa constrictor.

ARTIE: Does the school have money set aside to acquire a parakeet?

LEAH: Yes, it has a budgie budget.

Why did the snake have trouble speaking?

He had a frog in his throat.

How would you describe a nervous frog?

Jumpy.

Why don't snakes need eating utensils?

They already have a forked tongue.

When does the classroom mouse need oil?

When it starts to squeak.

What distinguishes one venomous snake from another?

Its poisonality.

ARTIE: Does the class boa love the students?
LEAH: Yes, it has a crush on them.

When is a frog happiest?

During a leap year.

What do you do if you find a deadly viper in your toilet?

You wait until he's finished.

Why do frogs make such great outfielders?

They're good at catching flies.

What do you say to a hitchhiking bunny?

"Hop in!"

What's the favorite dessert of the class's pet snake?

Mice cream.

ARTIE: What did the colorful little fish's mom cry out when her son brought home straight As from his school of fish?
LEAH: "Atta koi!"

Why do amoebas excel in math?
Because they're so good at multiplying and dividing.

RECESS, MORE OR LESS

What do the students in metrics class like to play at recess?
Follow the liter.

What do Thidwick and Bullwinkle enjoy playing?
Duck, duck, moose!

Why was the boy looking forlorn?
He had lost his marbles.

What do mice have fun playing?
Hide-and-go-squeak!

What do tugboats like to play?
Tug-of-war.

But how did the reluctant tugboat feel about it?
She thought it was a drag.

How do some students get their kicks during recess?

Kickball.

ARTIE: Was Frankenstein's monster brought back to life for a game of dodgeball?

LEAH: Yes, he was recess-itated.

Which board game do the students in Prague enjoy most?

Czechers.

What did the goat who picked on the other goats in the schoolyard become?

A bully goat.

What does your bottom get if you sit too long on a seesaw?

See-sore!

What can you find polar bears playing?

Freeze tag.

And how about the students in architecture school?

Frieze tag.

What do kids wear when playing Marco Polo?

Marco Polo shirts!

What do Irish Setters like to play?

Red rover.

What's the favorite playground game of kangaroos in kilts?

Hopscotch!

Who was all dressed in a black, black, black tuxedo?

Mister Mary Mack!

What are kiddie cars fond of playing?

Red light, green light.

What is it called when students replace each other on a hanging seat in the playground?

The swing shift.

Which uniform is best worn when playing jump rope?

A jumpsuit.

HA HA HA HA HA HA

What do students eat after playing four square?

A square meal.

What do twins from Amsterdam like to play?

Double Dutch.

What is it called when four people are playing cat's cradle?

A string quartet!

What favorite recess game pits carnivores against herbivores?

Tug-of-vore.

Which outdoor game do French schoolchildren love to play?

Kick the Cannes.

Which game features whoops of encouragement that abruptly stop?

Musical cheers.

ARTIE: What do Jill's BFF and the beanstalk boy enjoy playing?
LEAH: Jacks!

What was Dr. Jekyll's favorite recess activity?

Hyde-and-seek.

A FEW GOOD SPORTS

Who comes to school in a horse-drawn carriage?

The coach.

Which role does a sailor often take in baseball?

The on-deck hitter.

Why do quarterbacks succeed in school?

They're skilled at passing.

What soccer position do zombies usually play?

Ghoulie!

When is the outcome of a football game in the bag?

When the quarterback is sacked.

LEAH: Was the golf lesson about what you expected?

ARTIE: I'd say it was par for the course.

Who stopped to tweak the opposing third baseman while rounding the bases?

The pinch runner.

Who was the first mummy to play golf?

King Putt.

Why does it take so long to run from second to third base?

There's a short stop in the middle.

Where do the Chicago Eels play their home games?

Wriggly Field.

What's the favorite breakfast dish of defensive linemen?

The quarterback scramble.

Why did the simpleton bring earplugs to the tennis match?

He heard the players would raise a racquet.

What do you call an ungroomed infield?

A baseball diamond in the rough.

Which animals would gladly trade a bowl of milk for a bowling ball?

Alley cats!

How would you describe an angry golfer?

Teed off!

When Alexander Graham Bell played baseball, what was his best pitch?

The Bell curve.

What did the catcher say to the pitcher when the game had ended?

"Catch you later."

What do you call the money a tennis player earns?

Her net income.

HA

How many school coaches does it take to change a lightbulb?

None, because you can do it. *You can do it!*

Who occupies the deepest position in the defensive backfield on the school football team?

School safety.

Why do golfers always have an extra set of trousers?

In case they get a hole in one.

Who is the tidiest baseball player in the lineup?

The cleanup hitter.

Which popular team sport can be played with a stuffed stocking if a ball is unavailable?

Socker.

What phrase opens a match between fireflies?

"Ready, set, glow!"

Where is the best place to go to replace a worn-out soccer uniform?

New Jersey.

HA HA HA HA HA

What was Dracula after too many bites at the baseball game?

A full count.

Which pastries must the offense always avoid?

Turnovers!

What does a rude center say to his quarterback?

"Take a hike!"

What's the best way to teach someone how to steal a base?

A slide show.

Why wouldn't you want Cinderella on your baseball team?

She runs away from the ball!

Which position on the football team does the class dunce play?

Left back.

HA HA HA HA HA
HA HA HA
HA HA HA HA HA

MORE SCHOOL DAZE DOOZIES

Where does the homeroom teacher stand?

The home front.

What's the favorite school supply of farmers' children?

Pro-tractors!

Which writing implements do pigs and bulls prefer?

Pens.

In which place of learning do you have to practically bang on the door to get in?

The school of hard knocks.

How does a DC Comics superhero increase his vocabulary?

Flash cards.

Knock, knock.

Who's there?

Isador.

Isador who?

Is a door a door when it's ajar?

What do you call it when parts of your hair are straight and parts are curly?

Combination locks!

When is a large eraser healthiest?

When it's in the pink.

Where do low-ranking soldiers get an education?

Private school.

ARTIE: Would I be in trouble for something I *didn't* do?

TEACHER: Not at all. That wouldn't be fair.

ARTIE: That's good to know because I didn't do my homework!

Why do noses often drop out of school?

They get tired of being picked on.

HA HA HA HA HA

ARTIE: What work do you do year after year but never get paid for?

LEAH: Homework!

Where is the best place to learn to do sums?

Summer school.

Knock, knock.

Who's there?

Arthur.

Arthur who?

Arthur any other schools I can go to? This one has the silliest knock, knock jokes!

What's the perfect winter schoolroom beverage?

Hot chalk-olate.

Which degree is needed to become a letter carrier?

A *post*-graduate degree.

How would you describe students who have studied too hard for their French exam?

French fried!

Where do writers of verse go for shade and inspiration?

A poet tree!

What is used to sweep up a homeroom?

A home broom.

What goodies are brought to school in knapsacks?

Knap snacks!

Why are fish so smart?

They travel in schools.

LEAH: Do the best schools retain most of their teachers?

ARTIE: Yes, they still have all of their faculties!

Why did the student powder her nose during the test?

She was taking a make-up exam.

What are students given for getting a poor grade?

D-tention.

HA HA HA

Knock, knock.

Who's there?

Warren.

Warren who?

Warren you the student whose cat ate his homework?

Why did Emma's dog, Cosmo, have a big, round bulge in his tummy?

Because the dog ate her homework—and she was studying the globe!

Which instructional schoolbooks teach fictional excuses for why your homework never got done?

Pretext-books.

TEACHER: You missed school yesterday, didn't you?

ARTIE: Hmm, not really. Did it miss *me*?

What happened to the boy who was so absorbed in his book that he walked into a tree branch?

He became a leveled reader.

What is the favorite subject of many teenage girls?

Guy-ology.

HA HA HA

Who does a super job managing the school system?

The *super*-intendent.

TEACHER: Artie, what is the outermost layer of a tree called?

ARTIE: I'm afraid I don't know.

TEACHER: Bark, Artie. Bark!

ARTIE: *Woof woof woof!*

Why was the girl in a sticky situation at school?

Her glue bottle was leaking.

What does a minicomputer order for a snack?

A little byte.

Which lemon drink do educators turn to for refreshment?

Teacher's-ade.

Knock, knock.

Who's there?

Supplies.

Supplies who?

Supplies! Now let me in.

What do grammar teachers call Santa's helpers?

Subordinate Clauses.

Why are giraffes unable to focus in class?

Their heads are in the clouds.

ARTIE: Do ghosts attend school?

LEAH: Sure. Haven't you heard of school spirit?!

What do you call someone who finds going to classes tedious?

School-bored!

Why do music teachers suffer so?

They have more than their share of trebles.

What do you call assignments that pigs take home from school?

Hamwork.

LEAH: How old do students have to be to attend middle school?

ARTIE: Middle-aged!

Who can be found in the homeroom of a boys' school?

Homeboys!

Which breed of dog is best drawn with a Sharpie?

A Shar-Pei.

How do you remove marks made by crayons?

With cray-offs!

In which class do pigs study the world?

Gehography.

Which senior British student is nearly perfect?

A prefect!

What do you call a student who aces exams?

A quiz whiz.

What's the first step in getting a master's degree?

A master class.

Which two letters make up an entire piece of writing?

S A.

Why did the teachers all call in sick?

They had come down with a staff infection.

Where do you not find students with straight hair?

At an all-curls school.

TEACHER: Class, we will have only half a day of school this morning.
CLASS: Yay!!!!
TEACHER: We will have the other half this afternoon.

Which European city-state is governed by a principal?

The Principality of Monaco.

Knock, knock.
Who's there?
Anita.
Anita who?
Anita be on my way. I'm late for school!

HA HA HA HA HA

HA HA HA

Where did the boy who flunked out of Greek class find himself?

Up the Greek without a paddle.

What did the mama buffalo say when her boy went off to school?

"Bison!"

Where is the best place to learn how to become your political party's candidate?

At a primary school.

And where is the best place for a football player to learn how to succeed in the defensive backfield?

At a secondary school.

What do you build a school with?

A board of education.

What happened when a prankster tied his classmates' shoelaces together?

They took a class trip.

What's the biggest gamble in grade school?

The alpha bet!

Where do students learn the best way to spend their summer break?

At a vacational school!

What do you call a school official in charge of discipline who has a bad case of vertigo?

Dizzy Dean.

ARTIE: Which bus is found *inside* the school?
LEAH: A syllabus!

Which important skill will keep you from discarding garbage improperly?

Litteracy.

How do students learn to navigate a supermarket?

In shop class.

TEACHER: I hope I didn't just see you looking at Tommy's exam.

LEAH: I hope you didn't either.

Why didn't the Invisible Man go to the prom?

He didn't have any *body* to take.

In which preschool are children at their gentlest?

In a kinder-garten.

Who is in charge of all the chairs in school?

The chair leader.

What has fifty feet and sings?

The school choir.

Which breed of dog is most likely to eat your German homework?

A German shepherd.

Which flag flies over an academy for pirates?

The school-and-crossbones.

HAHAHA
HAHAHA

HA HA HA HA HA
HA HA HA HA HA
HA HA HA HA HA

LEAH: Did you hear about the music teacher who got locked inside the classroom?

ARTIE: No, but I bet his keys were inside the piano!

Knock, knock.

Who's there?

Gladys.

Gladys who?

Gladys the weekend. No school!

What was the pen doing by the windowsill?

Looking for a pen-sill.

What puts a hole in the school day?

A fire drill!

Where do budding dermatologists learn the basics?

Skin-dergarten.

What do fish study in music class?

Their scales.

What do elves have to work on after class?

Their gnomework.

When is a student submerged in failure?

When his grades are below C level.

Where do pupils learn the best
way to swap and barter?

Trade school.

Why did the broom flunk out of school?

It was always sweeping in class.

LEAH: How do you greet your
new school?
ARTIE: Hi, school.

In which class do you learn to count up
butterfly populations?

Mothematics.

What class are witches most fond of?

Spelling.

Why do English teachers benefit when they come
across a lowercase proper noun?

Because they capitalize on it.

Why do prisoners do well in English class?

They already know about sentences.

TEACHER: Are you good at chemistry?
ARTIE: Yes and no.
TEACHER: What do you mean "yes and no"?
ARTIE: Yes, I'm no good at chemistry.

What occurred when the wheel was invented?

A revolution.

TEACHER: Didn't I tell you to stand at the back of the line?
LEAH: You did. But there was already someone there.

What did the ghost teacher tell the class?

Just look at today's lesson on the board and I'll go through it again.

When is a chain edible?

When it's a food chain!

HA HA HA HA HA

How many tickles does it take to crack up a squid?

About ten tickles.

Why do you never find an elephant in computer class?

They're afraid of the mouse.

LEAH: What did you learn in school today?

ARTIE: We learned how to write.

LEAH: Well, what did you write?

ARTIE: I don't know. We haven't learned how to read yet.

What's the best thing about getting one-on-one instruction in school?

You're in a class of your own.

What did the music teacher use to fix the broken tuba?

A tuba glue.

Where do you learn pre-algebra?

Preschool.

HA HA HA

HA HA HA HA HA HA HA HA HA HA

Why are calculators so reliable?

Because you can count on them.

How do many students view puns?

As punishment!

What do you call a duck that excels in school?

A wise quacker.

Why did the playful aquatic mammal cross the river?

To get to the otter side.

How do you hear about exciting new ice cream flavors?

You get the scoop.

What kind of trousers does a brainiac wear?

Smarty pants.

Why did the boy bring a sweet dried fruit to the school dance?

He needed a date for the prom.

Why was the smart-alecky student's nose red?

He was the class clown.

Knock, knock.

Who's there?

From.

From who?

Actually, it should really be "from whom." So sorry!

LEAH: Did you hear about the big cow that rampaged through the school with the principal in pursuit?

ARTIE: It was a high-steaks chase!

How do students file into the auditorium for a schoolwide meeting?

In an assembly line.

Which toy spins in your lap?

A lap-top.

HA HA HA HA HA HA HA HA HA HA

Did the school superintendent do anything to repair the broken sidewalk?

Yes, he took concrete steps.

What do you get if you wear safety goggles in class?

Safety giggles.

Where in the classroom can you watch a cartoon about seven dwarves?

On the Snow Whiteboard.

Knock, knock.

Who's there?

Your pencil.

Your pencil who?

Your pencil fall down if you forget to wear a belt!

What do high school students sit in?

High chairs.

What does a sculptor leave behind?

A body of work.

HA HA HA

Why did the man who rented out his house never attend his classes?

He was an absentee landlord.

In which school are all the lessons somewhere between black and white?

Grayed school.

Why did the students in one schoolroom all look alike?

They were the class clones.

What do you do on a second-period exam when you don't know the answer?

You second-guess.

Who keeps all the teachers in line?

A staff sergeant.

Where do the students at boarding school live?

In a boardinghouse.

When is the most dangerous time for students to go ice-skating?

Winter break.

Knock, knock.

Who's there?

Orange.

Orange who?

Orange you glad school's out for the summer?!

Artie Bennett is an executive copy editor by day and a writer by night. In praise of his books for children, the *Huffington Post* wrote, "It appears there is no topic Mr. Bennett can't make funny and educational."

Artie is the author of a quartet of hilarious picture books: *The Butt Book*, winner of the Reuben Award; *Poopendous!*, his "number two" book; *Peter Panda Melts Down!*, an adorable departure from derrières and doo; and the explosively funny *Belches, Burps, and Farts—Oh My!* In addition to writing *The Universe's Greatest School Jokes and Rip-Roaring Riddles*, he is also the author of *The Universe's Greatest Dinosaur Jokes and Pre-Hysteric Puns*.

Artie and his wife, Leah, live in Brooklyn, New York, where Artie spends his time moving his car to satisfy the rigorous demands of alternate-side-of-the-street parking. Visit ArtieBennett.com . . . before someone else does!